At a Loss
How to Help a Grieving Friend

By
Steve Dehner

GREENTOWN PRESS

FOREST GROVE, OREGON

At a Loss: How to Help a Grieving Friend

www.atalossbook.com

Published by Greentown Press, Forest Grove, Oregon.
greentownpress.com

Cover design by Grant Hawley.

Dehner, Steve (Stephen Joseph), 1963 -
At a Loss: How to Help a Grieving Friend / by Steve Dehner
pages cm.
1. Grief 2. Bereavement

ISBN 978-1-7335174-0-9 (Paperback)

Printed in the United States of America.

For all our comforters

who walked with us and

taught us how to comfort others.

May you receive as much

in your hour of loss.

Teach me to feel another's woe...

—Alexander Pope,
"The Universal Prayer"

Table of Contents

1
First Things First

Can I see another's woe,
And not be in sorrow too?
Can I see another's grief,
And not seek for kind relief?
—William Blake,
"On Another's Sorrow"

Helpless.

That is the feeling when someone close to you desperately needs your help and you don't know what to do for them. That wall of helplessness is precisely what most people face when a friend or family member has lost a loved one, an event that casts them into the shadow-valley called grief. For those who find they don't know how to care for and support their grieving loved ones, it can feel like a failure of love or friendship—but it is not.

You Can Help

When someone suffers such a loss, many people may surround them, wanting to offer help but soon realizing that knowing what do or say—how to be their friend—is not always obvious. That is not because they are uncaring or insensitive. It's because they have never experienced this type of grief or this type of helping before, and it is all new to them. If you see yourself as one of these people, wanting to care for and support someone close to you but unsure how, this book will help.

Most books on grief are written for your grieving companion. Most of them are too long. Some of them tell stories so sad or traumatic that the reader might not get past the first few pages. It may be a while before they can even think, without sheer dread, about what lies ahead for them in their journey through grief.

But you can think for them.

At a Loss is for you, the companion who is not bereaved.

You likely feel some urgency in learning how to be a friend to someone in pain. This book is short and to the point. If you want something you can read in a day, that cuts to the chase and gives you what you need to know now, you're holding the right book. If you don't have the patience, or the time, or the emotional bandwidth for plodding though long, tragic, fluffy, or perhaps horrific anecdotes before getting to the information you need, you're holding the right book.

I write as someone who has experienced devastating loss, has recovered from grief, and through it all was blessed by the best friends and most caring community a person could ask for. In 2003, a teenage driver struck my wife and two oldest children as they were driving to school. We lost our son, Paul—two weeks before his fourteenth birthday, and the day before Thanksgiving. Our daughter, Elyse, almost died but finally woke up, though with life-altering injuries after ten weeks in a coma.

The following pages will help you help a friend, partner, relative, coworker, or classmate— anyone you care about—who has suffered the loss of someone they love. Some of what you learn here could possibly apply to different kinds of losses: the death of a pet, a divorce, an estrangement, permanent injuries, or the loss of parental custody, a job, or a career. While any of these may be an occasion for grief, here we will directly consider only the aftermath of human death.

Millions of people grieve every day, and for every bereaved person, there are those who are not grieving but want to help the one who is—

countless people at any given time. This book is for all of you who walk with the wounded and hurting so that you may give practical expression to your empathy and compassion.

Grief, when confronted and processed honestly, is not unnatural, unhealthy, or permanent. Rather, it is a normal response to a sad but inescapable event in every life. We should view it as a journey to travel, a path to take, and a season of life from which we may recover. With help, we can gain new strength, greater wisdom, and deeper compassion. On the other side of grief, there is peace again, and joy.

The first thing to know is this: you can help. You can make a difference. Your care for your companion, your willingness and availability, are the only prerequisites. It will matter that you are in your companion's life and that you will walk with them through this darkness

Your Greatest Help

The number one thing that you have to offer is neither skill, nor knowledge, nor experience. It is not the right words or an abundance of ideas.

It is your presence.

Simply being with your loved one: sitting, eating, praying, or walking—it doesn't matter what you are doing as much as it matters that you are there. Really there. I mean, settling into the emotional and spiritual place your companion is in. You can't necessarily feel their pain, but you can be with them in it.

Many of us naturally fear doing this, a trepidation that leads some to fail to show up for their bereaved friends. This fear comes from our dread of death. It comes from the terror of venturing into the darkness of the shadow of death, the place of anguish and helplessness. Some people avoid a grieving person for fear of not knowing what to say or do for them. Please remember this if you are tempted to judge or resent the friends or relatives who don't show up: the reason for it is probably this fear of death and pain most of us share. Another cause could be a past or present trauma or their own unresolved grief, which makes it impossible for them to reach out. They need our understanding as well.

But if you can reach out, do. In my experience, nothing dispels that fear better than drawing closer to the event with love and compassion. I have now seen several dying friends, sometimes at the end of a long and painful struggle, who embraced their passage from this world. Seeing them pass dispelled my fear of facing life's end.

I believe the force that truly opposes and overcomes fear is not bravery but love. If you are reading this now, you are probably not withdrawing; you want to choose love over fear. God bless you for that.

2
A Friend in Crisis

I will not say: do not weep; for not all tears are an evil.
—J. R. R. Tolkien, *The Return of the King*

Someone has died.

A parent, a partner, a sibling, a child, a close friend. Someone you care about is grieving this loss. And it is not safe to assume that that person knows how to grieve in a healthy way that will lead toward recovery. Even grieving well in the past does not always prepare us for a new and more severe loss. Though I grieved for my grandmother at age twenty-seven, that did not mean I knew how to grieve for my son thirteen years later. That second loss was different: it was deeper, and it was profoundly more devastating.

Responses to Death

Our culture is ill at ease with death and its aftermath. We fear it. We don't like to talk or think about our own mortality, and we keep the painful process of death and mourning well concealed behind closed doors—just as we do with the bodies of those who have passed. Because death and dying have become so private and so little discussed, we do not pass along the example or the wisdom of properly grieving and recovering from loss.

Put simply, most people in our society do not know anything about grief when they find themselves in it. Nor do their friends. Now you are one of these friends, and you need to know how to help. As you read on, you will gain a brief overview of what grief looks like, what to expect, and how you can offer support and comfort.

If You Are Grieving

In the previous chapter, I explained that the most important thing you can give your companion is your presence, being fully attentive and willing to listen. This will be hard to do if you are presently bereaved yourself. If you are also grieving a loss— the same loss as your companion or a different one—you should not take on the role of their primary support and comfort. You are not fully available to help them through their grief because you must tend to your own process, which requires your entire emotional, physical, and spiritual being. Do not think that you have enough left over for someone else—and please, do not be talked into giving so much, not yet.

I am not saying you should turn away from a friend in need. I am not saying you shouldn't spend time together. But understand that you are on a path yourself, and you must take it first. You have your work to do, and you must do it before you're ready to help others. Somewhere down this road, you'll be the best person to bring comfort and help, but first, you need to recover. Finish this book if you like, but I suggest giving it to one of your non-grieving friends, so they can help you!

Varieties of Grief

No two people grieve alike. Even if you have experienced grief or observed someone's bereavement before, it does not necessarily mean that it will resemble your companion's current situation. Losses have different dimensions, and so do our responses to them.

Sometimes death comes after an illness or injury and was therefore anticipated for some time. Others are terribly shocking. Death by suicide or murder can carry added wounds or trauma. Mass-casualty events such as natural disasters can mean grieving multiple losses. The nature of the relationship to the deceased can throw hurtful and conflicting emotions like regret, guilt, or shame into play.

Not all losses will be expected, and not all will bring you face-to-face with the worst of situations. But at the very least, you will be with someone in deep pain. This is another very crucial point: grief is normal and natural. It is the response of human beings to the loss of someone they love. Every person dies, and the people who love them will experience the sense of loss we call grief.

It is important not to rank losses or make assumptions or comparisons about the severity of the loss. Since my wife and I lost our son, we have heard statements such as "My loss is nothing compared to yours," or, "Losing a parent is at least natural; losing a child is not." Even though these are understandable thoughts, it is best not to say them, particularly if it means assessing your friend's grief as easier than someone else's. Everyone's loss bears enough sorrow, quite enough.

At the same time, I have heard some stories that are truly horrific. In these extremely heartbreaking situations—the loss of all or most of a family, for example—the fears I have mentioned are more likely to prevail, especially the worry that we will have no words, no gestures, and no means to truly help. If you have it within you to be the person who can face this darkness, even in silence, please do it. Be there.

Emotional Chaos

Grief is a tightly grouped and often chaotic constellation of strong emotions. This is important to keep in mind as you travel with someone on this journey. Along with sorrow, there may be any number of concomitant feelings, such as shock, anger, confusion, numbness, regret, emptiness, loneliness, fear, guilt, hopelessness, shame, denial, and vindictiveness. At the same time, a person may also experience gratitude, relief, and the bitter sweetness of happy memories.

It can be hard enough for the grieving to understand and cope with all these feelings. It can be that much harder for those around them, who can only watch their friend struggle under the tangled heap. I recall, in the days following the death of our son, coming to the sudden realization that my feelings had flown utterly out of my control. Some of them made no sense to me at first. For example, I found myself baffled by the recurrence of feelings associated with losses

17

throughout my life: when my parents divorced, when a close friend moved away, when a girlfriend broke up with me. It dawned on me I had not been able to grieve those losses because I knew nothing of the need to do it, nor how I could. Now that an H-bomb had fallen on me, I was standing at ground zero, stunned, and finding these long-ago losses among the ruins. I was falling under wave after wave of sorrow.

Remember, if it is disconcerting to observe someone in this state, just consider how it is for the person experiencing it. Again, the most important thing for you and them to know is that it is normal—all of it. Love plus loss equals grief.

And: it will pass.

We wonder how someone could feel this intense pain for any prolonged period. Well, they can't, and they won't. In the early days, the bereaved may not be able or even need to hear this, but if you know it, that can help. You will have patience and perspective. You do not need to share their dread of forever feeling this anguish. It will get better; then it will get worse. But your loved one will come out on the other end.

3
Understanding Grief

Sorrow makes us all children again—destroys all
differences of intellect. The wisest know nothing.
—Ralph Waldo Emerson, *Journals*

Grief is an onslaught of emotion in response to a
loss. It requires a person to adapt to a new set of
circumstances (which is the path of recovery) and
move toward a life in which they are at peace with
those circumstances and have established a life and
identity without the deceased person (which is
recovery from grief).

Layers of Loss

Usually, immediately after a death occurs, the
bereaved do not fully fathom all they have lost in
that person and their relationship with them. The
awareness of this unfolds over time, and each new
sense of loss is dealt with as it emerges. Because of
this, grief can actually worsen. This is some pretty
bad news. Even though it will not be true for
everyone, it's only fair to warn you of the
possibility.

When a person loses a parent, their entire lifetime with them has ended. For many, this also means that unresolved issues in the relationship can now never be addressed.

When someone loses a spouse or a child, that person loses the future that they would have enjoyed together, a whole lifetime of joys, sorrows, and milestones. It may mean never having grandchildren or never seeing the child graduate or marry. Losing a partner can mean becoming a single parent or never having children. The survivor's new life may now bear twice the responsibility, twice the work, and a huge gaping hole where the partner once was.

Your grieving companion probably will not sense all these losses right away. As they do, each one is a new and sometimes overwhelming hurdle. Each time it can feel like reopening a wound. This is where friends who are committed to them for the long haul make a significant difference.

Stages of Grief

The process of bereavement cannot be sorted into predictable phases that follow a pattern or sequence. The landmark 1979 book *On Death and Dying*, by Elizabeth Kübler-Ross, left a lasting impression on our society, even among those who never read it, that in facing our own impending death, we pass through a sequence of emotional stages including denial, anger, bargaining, depression, and acceptance. She and David Kessler went on to adapt these stages to grieving in *On Grief and Grieving* (2005). Even though their subtitle uses the misleading phrase *Stages of Loss*, the authors acknowledge that the stages do not follow a timeline. While understanding these responses can be helpful, thinking of them in such limited and organized categories can diminish the range of emotional chaos grief can bring on.

In fact, there is very little about grief that is predictable, and there is no foreseeable sequence. For example, with a son who was gone and a daughter hanging on to life by a strand, I was not in denial, nor was I angry or depressed. And while I prayed howling, desperate, and sometimes wordless prayers, I never bargained. Grief may present itself as a storm, a crushing weight, as a dark corridor, a cold abyss, or a wild fire. It will be a little different for every person and will change over time.

That does not mean we can't be prepared for what a person may experience. There are many things that are common to grieving. Knowing what they are can help us to understand them when they come.

Ups and Downs

Perhaps it seems like your companion has dropped into a hole, and they will gradually make their way up and out of it for good. Actually, grief is more like a roller-coaster ride, during which there are many precipitous drops and the climbs are much more gradual.

There may be shock at first, when the enormity of the loss has not made its full impact. This is a self-defense mechanism of the psyche but not necessarily denial. Waking up to the full reality could happen in a day or a week or may take much longer. When a person cannot, after considerable time, bring themselves to this reality, it is safe to say they are in denial. They have not accepted that the person has died and is gone from their life.

When the shock wears off, the first great downturn has arrived. Things may seem as bad as they can possibly be: the darkest, the saddest, and the longest of days and nights. This, in fact, may not be the case. There are many passages ahead, and some of them could feel worse: the memorial service and/or funeral; dealing with belongings; and holidays, birthdays, and anniversaries. For some people, the second year after a death is harder than the first.

But there will also be days that are not as bad. It may take a while, but eventually you'll see your companion smile or even laugh. Don't let observers misunderstand these periods of relief from constant pain. This does not mean the person is forgetting or ceasing to care about their loved one. The happy moments should be welcomed, and taken as a mercy, rather than as indications of a shallow, flip, or callous attitude.

Even with a healthy recovery, there is progress and there are setbacks, highs and lows, bad days and good. But over time, it is reasonable to expect the pain to diminish in its intensity and for there to be more good days than bad over longer stretches.

4
Recovering from Grief

Death has its revelations: the great sorrows which open the heart open the mind as well; light comes to us with our grief.
—Victor Hugo, *The Letters of Victor Hugo*

It is not true that time heals all wounds. If it were, the only thing we would need to do to heal would be to wait. Time is certainly necessary, but it is not the agent of healing. Time will not bring about the transformation and transition the bereaved must undergo. They will have to do the work and persevere through the journey. This will take time, but time alone is not enough.

Mapping Progress
Progress through grieving is complex. Without goals, and without grief counseling or a recovery group, many people will not know what to work toward, what to hope for, and what to expect. In our case, my wife and I did not have the benefit of that sort of help when our son died because we were preoccupied with helping our daughter recover from her injuries. Though we were deeply

cared for and supported, we also had little time or guidance for our grieving. My hope is that no one would face bereavement without compassionate guidance. Not because it cannot work—just as people grieve differently, they also recover differently—but because some of us will have greater trouble in traversing the wilderness of grief without the benefit of a map. Some will get lost.

However, with whatever resources they have, your companion should expect to notice some recuperation, such as a lessening of the intensity of painful or disruptive emotions, a return to managing their day-to-day affairs, and peace with themselves and others.

There is no way to predict how long this will take. For some people, it will take months or years. The time needed varies with the relationship, the manner of death, and other circumstances. As I have said, if all you do to help is be present, you are doing enough. Additionally, reading this book equips you to offer understanding and sensitivity as well as companionship.

If your companion finds that flying solo (with the support of caring friends) is not sufficient, they could be helped by a person or a group (or both) equipped to guide them through the process. That means someone who has specific training or experience helping the bereaved. They could be a psychologist or psychiatrist, a counselor, a spiritual adviser, or a coach. Preferably they will be trained in grief recovery, whether through a medical practice, counseling, or coaching. I would not recommend someone who regards grief as a spiritual malady or a mental illness. This does not mean I do not see a place in the grieving process for spiritual beliefs. I help in facilitating a faith-based recovery group and have heard repeatedly from the participants how helpful it is. Most of what is in this book that I did not learn from my grieving comes from several years of doing this. The privilege of helping others and hearing their stories has helped me to learn from the grieving of losses different from my own.

Goals

One of the things we do in group is present goals for the grief journey. They give focus and a way of tracking progress over time. They are not tasks to check off; they are things a person is moving toward that help that person recover. Why should you know about this? If you had a friend who was preparing to run a marathon, you wouldn't show up at their house with a gallon of chocolate ice cream and a dozen donuts. Why? Because you know what your friend's fitness goals are. In the same way, a sense of grief recovery aims will help you help your friend. Goals that you know about are goals you can support.

Acceptance is coming to terms with the permanent absence of the departed from this world. In whatever sense we believe their spirit or presence carries on, or doesn't, we must give way to their actual absence. Do they live on in our memories, in our hearts, in their legacies, and in the ways we were changed by them? Yes, but they are gone, and they are not coming back. We cannot hear from them, touch them, or have any ongoing relationship with them. Long-term refusal to face up to this truth will obstruct and delay recovery from grief. As hard as it may be, the one who grieves must let their loved one go from this life.

The *healthy expression of emotions* is a vital component of healing from grief. Dealing with emotions properly—honestly, authentically, and constructively—will help the bereaved to avoid the potentially destructive fallout from powerful, lasting, negative, and painful feelings. Lingering anger, resentment, or self-pity can hurt the person and damage their relationships. This means the person must be honest with themselves and others about what they are feeling, without guilt or shame, and express those feelings appropriately and hopefully without hurting others.

The realization of a new *identity* often follows the loss of a loved one. This is especially true with the loss of a partner but also applies to close friends, children, siblings, and so forth. The person left may no longer be a spouse, brother, sister, or parent. They may now be an orphan. Establishing and adjusting to a new identity is crucial to recovery.

That new identity should not include taking on the permanent role of "bereaved person." That is because a healthy identity is grounded in those things about us that are volitional (like relationships) or intrinsic (like ability), not things that have happened to us or people we have lost. Grief is not a sound basis for a new identity, because though it is profound, it is a life experience, and while the loss is forever, grief is not.

Spiritual goals, arising out a given faith tradition or practice, can make all the difference for those who have a clear understanding of how they connect with loss, suffering, and death. However, this can represent a crisis as well. A sudden tragic loss can present a challenge to deeply held expectations of providence, fairness, or happiness. Of course, this all depends on the spiritual beliefs of your companion. As a Christian, I sought God's comfort and presence, and I opened myself to what I could learn and how I could grow and change through my adversity.

Spiritual goals can encompass anything that draws a person into deeper faith, personal transformation, or living out more deliberately their values and beliefs in relation to themselves, others, or God. They could include things like deepening prayer life or meditation practice; fostering personal qualities such as forgiveness, compassion, generosity, or gratitude; or renewing a sense of purpose or aspiration. The person might attempt to clarify the meaning and impact of their loss (or suffering in general) on themselves, those they encounter, or humanity and the natural world. Seeing through the pain to a better day, to hope, and to renewal can be that light we all need when darkness descends.

5
Things That Help

Pity speaks to grief
More sweetly than a band of instruments.
—Bryan Procter, *The Florentine Party*

What are some things that can be helpful in grief, and how can you contribute?

A death can be so emotionally devastating and overwhelming that it takes a team, a network of help and support, to try to meet all the needs. People can be thoughtful and come up with many ideas, and at the same time, other things can fall through the cracks.

Don't expect your companion to know what they need or want, or what to ask for. Their mental fog may not allow it. Instead, make suggestions. For example, call and say, "I'm coming over. I'm bringing lunch," or, "Let's sort through your mail." If they know they don't want what you're offering, they can decline.

Here are common needs that start on the day of the loss, some of which will last for months or even years.

Emotional Support

Helping with Services

After the bereaved has attended to the body of the deceased, the first mountainous hurdle they face is the memorial service, the funeral, or both. When helping plan or execute the service, keep in mind how important this may be to everyone in the circle of the grieving, not only your companion. While everyone may feel strongly about it, it falls to the closest survivor, by blood or marriage, to decide how the services will be. Their wishes matter, so whoever is helping should strive to consult and communicate constantly, with sensitivity and grace. The people involved may be under great stress and not necessarily at their best.

Listening

Put simply, listen without talking. The hardest thing for almost anyone trying to comfort the grieving is not knowing what to say. The good news is that you truly do not need to say anything. Give them a shoulder to cry on and listen.

You can help this along by extending an invitation to your companion. Let them know you are available to hear what's on their mind. Offer to hear their story. Ask them if they want to share their feelings. You don't want to push them. Just open the door.

Sharing Memories

As much as possible, those in the company of the grieving who knew the deceased should offer to reminisce. People may assume that talking about the deceased is too painful for those who grieve, and in some cases that will be true, at least for a while.

However, for others, the opposite is often true. Sharing memories—happy, funny, and even bittersweet—is a tangible expression to the bereaved that, even though you don't feel it as intensely, you join them in feeling the loss as well, and you hold the memories dear. Stories and words of appreciation don't need to wait until, or end at, the memorial service.

Visiting

There will likely be times when they want visitors, but there is also the legitimate desire and need for solitude. When visits are welcome, don't be one of those who shy away out of fear of not knowing what to do or say. (That's why you're reading this book, isn't it?)

Helping Write a Grief Letter

A common struggle for grieving people is getting from others what they need that no one seems to recognize. Usually, the only way this can change is for the grieving person to communicate their wants and needs. This can be so hard. Telling someone, "No, I don't want you to bring everyone over. I need to be alone," or, "You may find me crying at my desk," each time it comes up can be logistically difficult, emotionally exhausting, and fraught with the constant risk of being misunderstood—especially when you can't anticipate your needs from day to day.

In our recovery group, we recommend writing a grief letter as a way of expressing what is needed and wanted. It can include:

• How the person is feeling in response to their loss

• What others may or may not expect from them

• What they find comforting at this time and what they do not

• A list of concrete, practical needs

All of these can change, and when they do, it's time to write a new letter. Writing a grief letter is something you can help with. Nowadays, a letter can be shared through email or social media. It can also be given to others to distribute—for example, to a supervisor at their work, a leader in their faith community, or a teacher or administrator at their school. For examples of a grief letter, see appendix 1.

Practical Support

Offering Meals

This is a very traditional and popular way of showing love and support for the bereaved. While nothing says "We love you" like a hot dish of comfort food delivered to the person's door, it helps to remember that some people in the throes of grief will have no appetite. As uneaten food accumulates, along with unretrieved dishware, meals may become more of a burden than a blessing. It helps to have one or two people coordinating meals, those who know what is needed. Smaller meals and portions, some that can be frozen for later, and less frequent meals (e.g., three times a week) over a long period of time may make sense as well.

Helping with Everyday Tasks
Some of us may feel we can do things like shopping, cleaning, or paying bills in our sleep, but not the grief-stricken. It may be a long time before these routine chores become manageable again.

See if your loved one needs help with household chores like laundry, cleaning out the refrigerator or the car, mowing the lawn or raking leaves, washing dishes, opening the mail, or putting away holiday decorations.

Providing Transportation
Driving your companion where they need to go can be helpful as well: the hospital, funeral home, doctor's or attorney's offices, and other errands. Grief can leave a person foggy and distracted and in no state to drive safely.

Encouraging Self-Care
By definition, self-care is the responsibility of the self, but a grief-stricken person could do with some encouragement and help. It could be something as small as providing bottled water, sitting with them in a park, or ensuring they have some healthy

snacks on hand. (Junk food will only aggravate the toll grief takes on the body, including the brain.)

There are four crucial components that sustain physical and mental health:

1. Hydration: drinking plenty of water
2. Diet: eating enough healthy food
3. Exercise: movement is good for the body, mind, and mood; doing it outside is even better
4. Sleep: As much as possible get it at night. Afternoon naps are fine, but can result in grogginess or disruption at night if they are too long or too late.

Grief is exhausting. It will deplete a person of physical and mental energy. When a person is at their lowest, taking care of basic physical needs is crucial. You can help by inviting your companion to go on a walk or hike, watching little ones so they can rest or sleep, or making sure they don't have to eat alone. Don't expect them to say yes. Just make the offer.

It makes sense for a person experiencing the stress of grief to see a physician. The effects of grief on the body can be potentially harmful, especially if there are other stress- or lifestyle-related medical conditions present.

As discussed in the previous chapter, I would not advise anyone to go through the journey of grief alone. Of course, some people are going to choose just that, relying on books and online help. However, they should be aware of the alternatives before going down that road. You can make suggestions, gather information for them, and perhaps offer to drive them to appointments or meetings. (One friend of mine even agreed to attend a grief recovery group with an acquaintance who was wary of participating—in the process, my friend discovered she needed to attend the group for her own recovery!) Ultimately, the person grieving must decide for themselves whether to seek guidance and help for what lies ahead. At the same time, they may come to sense such a need later. That's okay. It's never too late get help with recovery and healing.

6
Things That Can Hurt

Where grief is fresh, any attempt to divert it only irritates.
—Samuel Johnson, in Boswell's *The Life of Samuel Johnson, LL.D.*

At some point, every grieving person must contend with offensive or insensitive remarks or attitudes. It is the single most common complaint of the bereaved; these can cause pain second only to the loss itself. Even though it can be hard to do, I believe we should extend some understanding, even grace, toward those who wound with words or actions.

Dishonoring Grief

When people utter some of the nuggets listed below, they are usually displaying ignorance and ineptitude around loss and grieving, but not ill intent. They may be thinking selfishly, but they do not mean to hurt the grieving person. They usually think they are being helpful. I am listing these so that you won't try to help in a similar way. In addition, it may heighten your sensitivity to how others might speak into your companion's grief.

When I was hurting the most, I didn't have the emotional energy to get angry or resentful over such offenses, but I also didn't want to continue listening to them. Someone with tact and sensitivity can take on the role of "bouncer," running interference on situations that are more than the bereaved is up to dealing with. They may guard them from some of the following.

Being Derisive

The roiling emotions of grief can result in what onlookers would typically consider odd or irrational behaviors. Harmful actions aside, these should not be greeted with ridicule or disapproval. For example, a widower leaves all his wife's things exactly as she left them or keeps personal items as reminders, such as a hairbrush or a bathrobe. Small and normally meaningless objects can acquire significant associations and become invested with profound meaning. They remain as tangible links to the person who is now gone, to memories, and to personal, even intimate, shared moments.

Realize that some of the behaviors are sane and understandable, if strange, and may even help with healing. No one is being a friend who tries to make the bereaved feel silly or crazy at such times.

Offering Trite Sayings or Clichés
Hoo-boy. People say the darnedest things. Clearly, people who use these sayings don't recognize them as objectionable. How these saccharine or religious-sounding sentiments may strike someone who has just lost a partner or a child may not be obvious, but take my word for it: silence is better than just about anything people come up with to make things seem better than they could possibly be.

"There's a new angel in heaven now."

"God took her up to heaven because He wanted her with Him so badly/more than you did."

"The Lord giveth, and the Lord taketh away."

"At least we know he's in a better place."

The list goes on. "Everything happens for a reason." "It's all part of God's plan." These are known to have caused people to want to wring other people's necks. To the person offering them, there is undoubtedly wisdom and truth in these thoughts, but that is not the point. For the grieving, they are out of context, out of place. They can seem like easy bromides situated a comfortable distance from the anguish of grief. They can come across as shallow platitudes against deep sorrow. It is how a suffering person hears them that matters.

Trivializing the Loss
"You're young: you can still have another child/marry again."

"You'll find the strength you need to get through this."

"God never gives us more than we can handle."

"Time heals all wounds."

Rule out saying anything that tries to make the loss seem less than it is or easier to endure, or to make some kind of obvious sense of it. No one is trying harder than the bereaved is to make sense of it, and it is obnoxious to imply it's easy or obvious. This is nothing less than an assault on someone experiencing possibly the most excruciating emotions in their entire life.

Expecting Help or Support
When our loss had me utterly wrung out, I was baffled when a relative began to lean on me as though I were in a position to comfort or strengthen her. Obviously, I was not.

41

Later, I realized that when I saw myself as empty and frail, others saw me as strong. But I wasn't. Nobody should come to the grieving to draw strength. No matter how they seem, they are not available for that.

Suggesting Distractions
or Unhelpful Means of Coping
"Why don't you find something to keep yourself busy?"

"Take your mind off of it."

"Sounds like you need a drink."

There are things some people will do to avoid or medicate their pain. And while they may seem to make sense, they are ultimately hindrances to a healthy recovery from grief. One thing we do not want to do is recommend, endorse, or encourage those choices. This includes obsessively using work, busyness, recreation, entertainment, sex, drugs, alcohol, or any other substance or activity to numb or elude pain. Such means of coping only delay the inevitable emotional avalanche and debilitate people in coping in a healthy way. As those who love them, we don't want to do anything to nudge them toward this potentially destructive path.

Rushing Their Grief

One of the most common challenges for those who grieve is to hear from others questioning the time their recovery is taking. People unfamiliar with a healthy recovery (including the bereaved) do not realize how long it can take: months or, in many cases, years. What they are suggesting is that the grieving time is up. They may ask, "Isn't it time you move on?" or, "Aren't you over that yet?" or say, "It's time to get on with your life." The one who grieves is entitled to however much time they need to recover fully. Neither they nor anyone else can set a deadline for this.

Impatience with grieving can be subtle—acting surprised at the bereaved's sudden outburst of emotion, for example—or more intrusive: someone may take it upon themselves to claim, store, or discard belongings of the deceased or to alter their living spaces when it is not their prerogative to do so. This can be hurtful and disruptive for the grieving and damaging to relationships. The motive might be to move the grieving process along, but these can be immensely significant milestones on the grieving person's journey, and they must come to them when they are ready.

7

The Long Haul

> She was no longer wrestling with the grief, but
> could sit down with it as a lasting companion and
> make it a sharer in her thoughts.
> —George Eliot, *Middlemarch*

This book is about being a friend in the darkest hour, about showing up when it matters most.

Commonly, there is much support early on for those who are grieving. At the very least, there are the customary expressions of sympathy and offers of help. Over time, they subside. Friends and family will go on with their day-to-day lives, most likely with the mistaken belief that the worst part of the grieving is over.

It's not.

Some of the saddest, bleakest, emptiest days lie ahead. The grieving person still needs caring companions for the journey. Often, when they hit a new low in the valley of the shadow, they are alone. This is perhaps when they cast about for a support group or a counselor, but they still need their friends. The loss of friendships is an additional casualty they shouldn't suffer.

How can you help with the long-term recovery? Simply by continuing to care for your loved one as you have from the outset, by not assuming that all is well, by understanding the ups and the setbacks, and by recognizing the new experiences of loss along the way.

Most of all, you will help by continuing with them through the good and the bad, the joys and the sorrows.

Signs of Recovery

How will you know if your companion is recovering? Ultimately, it is beyond your control, and you will probably not know all the ins and outs of how they are progressing. Yes, they will continue to need support and love, but recovery—doing the work, enduring the long, bumpy ride—is the responsibility of the one who is grieving.

Nevertheless, because you care, you want to know that they are moving generally in a forward direction. You look forward to the day when a sense of peace and well-being returns and they can fully live life again.

With what I have learned from my own experiences and those of many others, I can usually recognize whether someone I know seems to be making a healthy recovery or not. I can spot many of the things they are doing that are helping or hindering. It is wonderful to see progress. It pains me to see a standstill.

Typically, if you observe the following *over time*, you are seeing progress:

- Fewer bouts of weeping or tearfulness
- A leveling out of emotions
- Fewer bad days, more good days: able to get up and out, make plans, get through a workday, take care of themselves, etc.
- Getting recovery help, if they sense that they need it
- Having and working toward grief goals (see chapter 4): accepting their loss, expressing their emotions, establishing a new identity, and setting or even meeting one or more spiritual goals
- Returning to previous patterns of sleeping and eating
- Regaining the ability to smile and laugh

Signs of a Rut

As I have said, bad days, setbacks, and ambushes are normal. However, while a person should give themselves permission to grieve, indulging certain behaviors can forestall recovery. These factors can point to a recovery that has not begun or has halted in its progress.

Seeking Attention

Some people find themselves in the spotlight after a loved one dies and then choose to stay there. That won't happen if they are seen making progress. Seeking attention long beyond the death provides the grieving a temptation to carry on indefinitely as if the loss occurred yesterday or to constantly hold up reminders (pictures, stories, achievements) of the deceased as if they never died. Social media is especially accommodating to the person hungry for continued attention.

Self-Medicating

These are things done usually to numb the pain and fill the void. As I discussed in chapter 6, legitimate pleasures, responsibilities, or medications can become the enemies of grief recovery: work, busyness, recreation, entertainment, food, sex, drugs, and alcohol, when used to avoid pain, do not and cannot further one's progress. In fact, used in this way, and to excess, they will delay it.

Denying the Loss
This is a conscious or unconscious refusal to accept that the person who died is gone and is not coming back. This can be a very delicate topic, tied as it often is to spiritual beliefs about the afterlife. However, regardless of beliefs, facing death requires at least an acknowledgment from your loved one that the person *as they knew them and related to them* is no longer here. Denial will prevent the adjustments needed for a new life and identity.

Nursing Negative Feelings
Self-pity, anger, resentment, vindictiveness, jealousy, envy—while these can be understandable responses to loss, nursing them and clinging to them will eventually take a counterproductive toll. Healing can only come after letting go of destructive thoughts and attitudes and resisting the urge to lash out against those believed to have caused harm during the grieving. They damage or

destroy relationships, which will only add to the loss.

How do you help your companion with these daunting and sensitive problems? First, realize that it not your responsibility to change their thinking or behavior. It could be hard enough just helping them to see a problem or how it might be hindering their progress. It might be easier and make more sense to steer them to a professional.

Second, remember to be patient and understanding. Denial, at least for a while, is a normal coping strategy, giving a person time to accept a difficult reality. If they are stuck there, you might try asking questions like, "Do you think it's completely sunk in yet that Janet is gone?" "I've heard that acceptance is necessary for healing. What do you think about that?" "What do you think it means to accept that Joe is gone? What do you think that would feel like?" A similar approach could work with other problem areas: asking exploratory questions and wondering with them if their coping strategies are working as hoped or are leading to healing.

It's Never Too Late to Begin Recovering

Even if some time has passed without having begun a grieving process (what I have been calling recovery) or if progress has stalled—it's never too late to begin the journey. I've known people who have struggled for their entire lives—twenty, thirty, or forty years—with grief they never properly processed, and a group program finally helped them. One such friend grew up with a mother who never could accept her husband's early death. Because she couldn't grieve, neither could her children grieve. Years later, that same mother refused to accept or acknowledge the suicide of one of her daughter's, my friend's sister. The mother forbade discussion of this tragedy as well, and if it ever came up, she only permitted it to be called a murder. My friend never properly grieved these losses, of her father and sister, mostly because it was not permitted in her family. It was decades later, when she attended a group, that my friend was finally able to revisit these losses and find healing.

I encourage anyone in a situation like this to take a courageous step (even if it is simply getting a good book on grief) toward recovery and healing.

Thank you, reader, for caring enough about your companion to walk with them through what can be a very difficult and heartbreaking ordeal. Thank you for teaching yourself how to better care for them. If anything could be considered a true test of love, patience, understanding, and kindness, it is your answering the call to help someone who is suffering from a great loss.

Appendix 1

Grief Letters

In chapter 5, I discussed the writing of a grief letter. In our recovery group, we recommend this as a way for grieving people to communicate with others how grief is affecting their daily lives and how the addressees can help them. To give you an idea of how to help a friend to compose a grief letter, here are a couple of sample letters.

Sample Grief Letter #1

In this letter to his boss, a widower explains what he is experiencing and how it may affect him in the workplace. He gives an idea of what people can expect when he comes back to work and asks repeatedly for patience and understanding. Finally, he explains how people who want to can help him practically.

Dear Liz,

First, I'd like to thank everyone at the office who sent gifts and cards. It means a lot.

Last time we talked, you asked how you and my coworkers could help when I return to work Monday. Thanks again for asking. I've written a few things down, with the idea that you could forward this by email to everyone:

Up front, I want to say that even though I am resuming work, I am not recovered from the loss of my wife, Ann. Twenty years of marriage coming to such an abrupt and painful end is not an easy loss, and it will be some time before the skies clear. I am very sad. I still cry every day. Often, it's all I can do to get through the day.

I am asking for your patience with me. I may cry at my desk. Please don't worry about me. Please understand, I don't have these emotions quite under control yet. I am distracted at various times. Like you, I am concerned how this may affect my work. I may need a little more time than usual to finish things. I may need to take a few extra breaks.

Liz and I have an agreement to try this out, and if I need to take some extra time off, I'll be able to. Most likely, that will mean working half days. I hope this doesn't make extra work for my team, but it probably will. Again, I ask for your patience.

I have learned in the last few weeks that everything I am experiencing is normal, so you needn't worry about me. But please know that this will take some time for me to get through.

I have also learned that some people are uncomfortable around me and don't know what to say. Please understand that you do not need to say anything. I appreciate your sympathy and concern, but I don't expect everyone to verbalize it. If you would prefer to write, I still like getting notes and cards. But it would be nice if I didn't feel people were avoiding me or walking on eggshells.

Someone asked if there was anything practical that I need. The meals that people were bringing have been a big help, especially with two teenagers waiting for dinner when I get home. If anyone wants to continue with the sign-up Liz started, then I can just take dinner home with me from here. That would be a great help.

Thanks again.

Sample Grief Letter #2

Here, a mother writes to a third-grade teacher on behalf of her daughter who has lost her father. Although she is speaking for someone else, she follows the same pattern: what her daughter is going through, how it may affect her behavior and performance, and how others can help.

Dear Ms. Griffith,

Thank you for your call the other day. Here is the note I promised, in the hope that it will help you and Keri's class with her return to school.

Obviously, this has been a very difficult time for Keri—and the rest of us. Our counselor has told me that what she is feeling and expressing is appropriate and to be expected with the loss of a parent. She is very sad. She also has been uncharacteristically short with her little brother. I am certain it's an expression of anger, which is also normal. We are all heartbroken, devastated. I know you can understand how hard it is to see my little girl in such pain. She tends to have her times of crying—sobbing, really—a couple of times a day, and then she recovers and is surprisingly okay afterward. I think you may find that she's having a hard time focusing on work and is working more slowly than usual.

She is worried about having a crying spell in the classroom—embarrassing for her, and disruptive and upsetting for her classmates. What if you had a little chat with her in the morning and let her know it's okay to excuse herself from the room when she feels a cry coming on? Could she do that?

Other than that, I think she would like everything to be normal. She doesn't like to be the center of attention, and she's been getting a lot of that lately. I don't know if you will see the little flashes of anger I've seen at home. But if you do, please be understanding. She is a very hurt little girl.

I am thankful that she has such a caring teacher! Please don't hesitate to call and let me know how things are going.

Appendix 2
Depression and Trauma

1
Depression: Mood or Mental Illness?

We often refer to a sad or unhappy mood as depression. However, moods are usually a response to our circumstances and eventually pass. When grieving, a person may feel this almost constantly.

As a mental or mood disorder, however, depression is a serious and potentially life-threatening mental health condition that can have a number of emotional or physical causes, and it does not pass in a few hours or days. Such depression, usually called clinical depression or major depressive disorder, is a prolonged state of gloom, sadness, apathy, and negative feelings turned in on the self. It can lead to suicidal feelings and plans, and a person experiencing it needs treatment by a medical professional.

Depression shares many symptoms with grief, which can make it difficult to discern whether a bereaved person, experiencing what is normal and healthy, has slipped into depression, which is neither normal nor healthy. Grief by itself is not a mental health disorder. Therefore, neither a provider nor a grieving person should treat it as one. They should not seek a pharmaceutical remedy (although symptoms like insomnia may require it). Depression, however, calls for a medical diagnosis and professional treatment. In some cases, grief can lead to depression. This would most likely happen in people who have had major clinical depression before or who reject or can't find support in their grief. Isolation is a key factor in grief sliding into depression, and while every grieving person needs time alone, they also need company.

Symptoms

According to the Mayo Clinic, depression's symptoms "occur most of the day, nearly every day" and may include:

- *Feelings of sadness, tearfulness, emptiness or hopelessness*
- *Angry outbursts, irritability or frustration, even over small matters*
- *Loss of interest or pleasure in most or all normal activities, such as sex, hobbies or sports*
- *Sleep disturbances, including insomnia or sleeping too much*

- *Tiredness and lack of energy, so even small tasks take extra effort*
- *Reduced appetite and weight loss or increased cravings for food and weight gain*
- *Anxiety, agitation or restlessness*
- *Slowed thinking, speaking or body movements*
- *Feelings of worthlessness or guilt, fixating on past failures or self-blame*
- *Trouble thinking, concentrating, making decisions and remembering things*
- *Frequent or recurrent thoughts of death, suicidal thoughts, suicide attempts or suicide*
- *Unexplained physical problems, such as back pain or headaches*[1]

Differentiating Depression and Grief

As you can see, if someone was suffering their grief at its greatest intensity, it would be hard to distinguish the symptoms from those of depression.

---

[1] This list was quoted exactly from: "Depression (Major Depressive Disorder)," www.mayoclinic.org/diseases-conditions/depression/symptoms-causes/syc-20356007. Accessed October 28, 2017. Used with permission of Mayo Foundation for Medical Education and Research. All rights reserved.

So, how can we tell if grief has turned into clinical depression? With mild depression, it is probably not possible, because it shares so many symptoms with grief. "Mild" refers to the condition that is not so severe as to affect the day-to-day activities of the person suffering it. I have already noted that it is usually the case that grief will affect daily activities at least some of the time. However, as you have now read, there are symptoms that stand apart from typical grief: for example, "Feelings of worthlessness or guilt, fixating on past failures or self-blame." When someone is experiencing negative feelings turned inward and that have little or nothing to do with the person who died, it points to possible depression. Depression will focus a person's thoughts on themselves. Things like happy memories or the sadness of the loss will not affect it. It will have a life of its own. Consequently, a depressed person cannot just shake it off. They need help.

The one thing that will most clearly bring depression into focus when a person is also grieving is time. With recovery from grief, the symptoms will gradually diminish until most of the physical and emotional stability returns to what it was before the death. This is not so with severe and untreated depression. Except for a type called atypical ("not typical"), depression is unrelenting ("most of the day, nearly every day") and often worsens over time. It is cruel, and it can kill.

What if your grieving companion is not working toward recovery? What if they are stuck? In that case, you will not see such a diminishment of grief symptoms, so how can you know if there is a clinical depression? It will be very difficult unless you begin to observe or suspect the following. These are clues pointing to depression distinct from grief, as taken directly from depression expert and health educator Nancy Schimelpfening:

- *Feelings of guilt not related to the loved one's death*
- *Thoughts of suicide—although in grief there can be thoughts of "joining" the deceased*
- *Morbid preoccupation with worthlessness (grief does not usually erode self-confidence)*
- *Sluggishness or hesitant and confused speech*
- *Prolonged and marked difficulty in carrying out the activities of day-to-day living*

- *Hallucinations and delusions; however, some people in grief may have the sensation of seeing or hearing the dead person*[2]

If there is any question of problems that go beyond grief, the best course is to see a health care provider who understands both depression and grief.

2

Trauma: An Assault on the Psyche

A person can experience trauma along with grief if they experienced or witnessed a terrifying event in connection with the death: if they witnessed the death or found the body afterward; if murder, suicide, natural disaster, mass killing, or grisly accident was the cause; if the way they learned of the death was especially shocking; or if the survivor contributed in some way to the cause of death. Any of these can cause devastating impacts on the brain, quite beyond the control of the person suffering them.

---

[2] Nancy Schimelpfening, "How Do You Know If It's Grief or Depression? Understanding the Differences," www.verywell.com/grief-and-depression-1067237. Accessed October 28, 2017. Used with permission.

Some people—but not all—who experience emotional trauma will suffer lasting symptoms. In medical terminology, these symptoms together can form post-traumatic stress disorder (PTSD). Just because a person has some of these symptoms does not mean they have PTSD (which also calls for a professional diagnosis), but they certainly are complicating factors in grief recovery.

Symptoms of PTSD

Again, not everyone who experiences trauma will have PTSD, but it doesn't hurt to know the symptoms. According to the US Department of Veterans Affairs' Center for PTSD, there are four types of PTSD symptoms (quoted exactly):

1. Reliving the event (also called re-experiencing symptoms)
Memories of the traumatic event can come back at any time. You may feel the same fear and horror you did when the event took place. For example:

- *You may have **nightmares**.*
- *You may feel like you are going through the event again. This is called a **flashback**.*
- *You may see, hear, or smell something that causes you to relive the event. This is called a*

trigger. News reports, seeing an accident, or hearing a car backfire are examples of triggers.

   2. ***Avoiding situations that remind you of the event***

> You may try to avoid situations or people that trigger memories of the traumatic event. You may even avoid talking or thinking about the event. For example:

• You may avoid crowds, because they feel dangerous.

• You may avoid driving if you were in a car accident or if your military convoy was bombed.

• If you were in an earthquake, you may avoid watching movies about earthquakes.

• You may keep very busy or avoid seeking help because it keeps you from having to think or talk about the event.

   3. ***Negative changes in beliefs and feelings***

The way you think about yourself and others changes because of the trauma. This symptom has many aspects, including the following:

• You may not have positive or loving feelings toward other people and may stay away from relationships.

- *You may forget about parts of the traumatic event or not be able to talk about them.*
- *You may think the world is completely dangerous, and no one can be trusted.*

4. ***Feeling keyed up (also called hyperarousal)*** *You may be jittery, or always alert and on the lookout for danger. You might suddenly become angry or irritable. This is known as hyperarousal. For example:*

- *You may have a hard time sleeping.*
- *You may have trouble concentrating.*
- *You may be startled by a loud noise or surprise.*
- *You might want to have your back to a wall in a restaurant or waiting room.*[3]

Helping Someone with PTSD

The good news is that most people can recover from even severe trauma. However, they likely will need some professional care and treatment. It is wise to seek help from a professional who has experience treating psychological trauma and PTSD and to do so as early as possible.

---

[3] National Center for PTSD, "Symptoms of PTSD," https://www.ptsd.va.gov/public/PTSD-overview/basics/symptoms_of_ptsd.asp. Accessed February 1, 2018.

Daniel K. Hall-Flavin, MD, of the Mayo Clinic has some suggestions for helping someone with post-traumatic stress (these are direct quotes):

• *Be willing to listen, but don't push. Make sure your loved one knows that you want to hear about his or her feelings. But if the person isn't ready or willing to talk about it, don't push. Just reassure your loved one that you'll be there if and when he or she is ready.*

• *Choose a time to talk. When you're both ready to talk, choose a time and place where you'll be free of distractions and interruptions. Then truly listen. Ask questions if you don't understand something. But avoid any urges to second-guess, to give advice or to say, "I know just how you feel."*

• *Recognize when to take a break. If you sense that the conversation is becoming too intense for your loved one, provide him or her with an opportunity to stop for now and take up the conversation again on another day. Then follow through.*

• *Get help if talk of suicide occurs. If your loved one talks or behaves in a way that makes you believe he or she might attempt suicide, respond calmly, but act immediately.*[4]

---

[4] Daniel K. Hall-Flavin, MD, "Post-Traumatic Stress: How Can You Help Your Loved One?" www.mayoclinic.org/diseases-conditions/post-traumatic-stress-disorder/expert-answers/post-traumatic-stress/faq-20057756. Accessed October 28, 2017. Used with permission of Mayo Foundation for Medical Education and Research. All rights reserved.

Postscript
Recovery, Ten Years Later

After reading these pages, you will have gleaned some of my story of loss and recovery. In 2014, I wrote an essay[5] that in part serves as a snapshot of life ten years after and in another way is a reflection on the process of recovering from our losses. I include it here as a way of pointing toward the future and saying, "They can make it—your companion can make it." Even the worst kind of loss is survivable. Not only survivable; they can come out on the other end actually enjoying life once again, experiencing peace, and finding greater strength and compassion within themselves.

---

[5] The essay, "What a Stone Weighs," first appeared in *Eclectica Magazine*, vol. 19, no. 3.

What a Stone Weighs

After driving a thousand miles from Southern California up to our small town on the northwest edge of Oregon's Willamette Valley, a large delivery van pulled up in front of our house. As Laura and I stood near our front door looking out, the van arrived at just the day and time it was supposed to.

Stepping out onto the large concrete porch, we watched as the driver put a small pallet with a package onto a dolly.

"Where would you like it?"

"Right here," I said, "on the porch."

"You sure?" Laura asked me.

"Yes."

I watched the driver closely as he set it down. His eyes avoided mine, and his smile came and went a few times, friendly but a little nervous. I wondered if that was his personality, or if it was the package. Did he know what it was? He must have.

"Do you know how much it weighs?" I asked.

"Two hundred pounds."

There was a time, a long time, when the weight seemed infinite, too heavy to contemplate. But that time had passed as we took delivery of a headstone for our son.

More than once in the ten years since Paul died—in a wreck the day before Thanksgiving—more than once we had tried to take up the task of getting a marker in place. It was a task made of smaller ones that were not small but mountainous, and at first we could not begin to think of tackling them. The first attempt came only two months after the funeral. I picked up a catalog of headstone designs from the funeral home. The first task, we supposed, was choosing a design, then the words, then the color of stone. At our dining table I opened the catalog to the section for children and infants. After browsing through pictures and sentiments for lost boys and girls, I brushed my tears from the pages, closed the catalog, and returned it.

A year or more later, Laura did the same. Looking at gravestones for children, it turns out, is not chicken soup for the soul. The weight of the stone, our stone, was more than we could lift. The weight was not the mass-times-gravity of a chunk of granite cut from a quarry in Vermont. Instead, that heaviness was our grief—which felt like our hearts cut from inside of us, broken, crushed. *Can we possibly find words for this anguish? Then let those stand as the stone-etched words to mark his grave.*

We did not go back to the catalog. Instead, we considered what the stone should say. For me, this was the real difficulty. Paul lived for just a little less than fourteen years. But a headstone, this stone, is supposed to say something about the person buried beneath it. A headstone is a memorial, after all. But how could we choose only a few words, a single phrase that can remember the person who is Paul Dehner—his clever and inventive mind, his humor, his friendships, his faith and love? The thought of having to find and settle for those words sickened me a little. I didn't want to do it. And not wanting to, unable to bring myself to it, I didn't, for ten years.

By endowing it with so much, I was standing on the stone, adding to its weight, and the stone would never become lighter.

But over time, the burden was lessened. We saw that the marker did not need to carry a lifetime. It did not have to hold memories, or stand for love.

A slab of granite, it would mark a place, a temporary place, an allotment of the earth given to hold and receive a body back to itself—but not Paul himself, who lives forever, whose memories are kept by God, who is missed in ways that can never be committed to a few, bitterly few, words.

The stone became lighter, as eventually we came to see that setting the stone was a small thing, or at least, small enough. We die, and most of us are forgotten when everyone who knows us has also died. The memory of my lifetime can only outlive me by less than a hundred years. Then, the living will pass by my gravestone looking for a different, fresher one. Someone may look at my grave and wonder who is buried there. The stone will be there to tell them. For those who know the deceased, it marks a place to visit, to remember, to mourn. That's all.

Ten years later, we are ready to place the stone. Today the funeral man came and took the stone away, and in a few days we will meet at Paul's grave to set it in the ground.

We ordered the stone from a company in California. We chose the words, and then the design, and then the color. Laura did most of the initial work, consulting my mom, and asked me to select a verse of Scripture.

Finally we chose the kind and color of granite. The finished stone is of flat red granite with Paul's name on top and a Celtic cross centered beneath. On either side are the dates. Recalling his love of performing, instead of saying, "Born" and "Died," Laura wrote, "Opening Night" and "Final Bow." Across the bottom, in italics, from First Corinthians 2:9:

No eye has seen,
no ear has heard,
and no mind has imagined
the things God has prepared for
those who love Him.

Hillside Cemetery lies seven miles north and mountain-ward from our town, on the gentle slopes rising to the Coast Range, founded in 1887 by pioneers who settled the area, and whose descendants still manage and care for it. Among them are some friends who offered us a plot when we suddenly needed one ten years ago.

We drove out with our daughter, Elyse, to find a man about our age, the funeral man, finishing the work. A couple of shovels and half a bag of sand lay between him and the open tailgate of his pickup. A mist of rain lighted on us and a mild wind swept the slopes. Kneeling in the well-soaked turf, he poured water across the shiny face of the slab, and brushed off the sand that framed it in the ground.

Laura asked him about caring for the stone, and he explained that keeping the engraved portions clean with a brush was most important. He also talked about how long the painting in the lettering should last—about five to ten years, after which it could be re-painted if we like. But the stone, and the inscription, they would last forever. Or, I thought, as close to forever as anyone would care about.

We talked about our own arrangements. I want a burial, Laura cremation.

"Have you thought about a green burial?" he asked me. "If you're environmentally conscious. No casket, no box, just wrapped in a shroud and put in the ground."

Laura was surprised that it was legal to do that. Not in the city limits, he said, but out here, it is.

"Oh, yeah," I said. "I think I'd like that."

Then he explained the downside to cremation.

"It has a huge carbon footprint, because it uses so much fuel. If you drove an SUV from here all way across the country, to DC, then drove back as far as Colorado, you would burn the amount of fuel it takes to reduce a single body to ashes."

In the course of talking, as we stood next to Paul's grave, and he stood over the stone, the man mentioned that he'd also lost his son. Yet, apart from muttering, "I'm sorry," which I don't think he heard, none of us offered our sympathies, and I thought it was odd, a funeral director not offering any condolences. Until it occurred to me, looking at the dates carved in the granite: it's because it's been so long.

Ten intervening years. The lightening years, the softening, normalizing, easing years. They were long and hard—long enough, I suppose, that condolences might not be thought in order. Long enough that the sorrow is not such a stabbing pain. They were years that could bring devastated parents to smiling and laughing at the graveside where on that ever-receding day they had wept inconsolably, canopied from a downpour.

Now we listen as the funeral man tells of disinterring someone who died in 1968— "There was nothing left of him except a few vertebrae. But his polyester suit and tie were good as new: they were perfect."—and we all laugh.

We tried to remember how Paul had been dressed, but couldn't be certain—another memory lost in the awful, swirling haze of grief over a son lost and a daughter yet in a coma. We remembered the simple but beautiful wooden casket a friend had made, Paul's youth leader at church, and how Paul's friends had gathered together to write messages on the inside of the cover: words of love and sorrow and farewell.

Though our grief has lightened over years, it's still heavy, hard, sharp around the edges, and insoluble against the years of our remaining lifetimes. As in the setting of the stone, our heartache becomes a lighter, a bearable sorrow, as heaven heals us.

Planted in the dirt and grass, the marker is surrounded by the life of the ancient hills draped with bean-rows and vineyards, evergreens and yearly-renewed flora—life that stubbornly goes on, indifferent to death or graves, to past pains and sorrows. Grief can look like this: it moves slowly, and some days not at all, as life and the world go on their way.

Though it was long in coming, the headstone was made and set in the ground at just the right time. And it will outlast us all, past the day that each of us who knew Paul in this world will greet him with inexpressible joy in the next, lighter than light.

Key Points from Each Chapter

Chapter 1: First Things First

- This book intends to help you help a friend, partner, relative, coworker or classmate—anyone you care about—who has suffered the loss of someone they love.

- Grief, when faced directly and processed honestly, is not unnatural, unhealthy, or permanent.

- Grief is a normal response to a normal and inescapable, albeit sad, event in every life. So, we should view it as a journey to travel, a path to take, and a season of life from which we may recover.

- Your love and support can make a difference in a person's recovery.

- The most important thing you have to offer is your presence.

Chapter 2: A Friend in Crisis

- To grieve is the normal human response to loss.

- Besides sorrow, it can include many different emotions.

- The intensity of the pain a person feels at its worst will lessen.

Chapter 3: Understanding Grief

- Grief brings an onslaught of emotions.
- When a death first occurs, the bereaved often do not yet fully fathom all they have lost.
- Grieving can actually worsen at some point down the line than it was at first.
- The process of bereavement cannot be sorted into predictable phases that follow a pattern or sequence.
- There are a great many things that are common to grieving and knowing about them can prepare us.
- Even with a healthy recovery, there is progress and there are setbacks, highs and lows, bad days and good.

Chapter 4: Recovering from Grief

- It is not true that time heals all wounds.
- Without help navigating grief, many people become lost.
- The grieving should have help from a person or a group (or both) equipped by experience or training to guide them through the process. It could be a psychologist or psychiatrist, a counselor, a spiritual adviser, or a coach.

- Grief should *not* be treated a spiritual malady or fault.
- When depression or some other complicating mental health issue is not present, grief should *not* be regarded or treated as mental illness.
- Suggested goals for the grief journey: acceptance, healthy expression of emotions, establishment of a new identity, and spiritual goals.

Chapter 5: Things That Help

- Don't expect your companion to know what they need or want, or what to ask for.
- It can take an entire team, a network of help and support, to try to meet all the needs of the bereaved.
- If helping to plan or work on the funeral or memorial services, give sensitive consideration to the wishes of those closest to the deceased.
- You don't need to know what to say. You can just listen.
- If you have them, and they are welcome, share memories of the person who is gone.
- Visit when the grieving wants company; refrain when they do not.

- Help write or distribute a grief letter. See appendix 1 for examples.

- Prepare and deliver meals or coordinate others to do so. Do not over-provide.

- Help with shopping, housekeeping, yard work, mail, or paying bills.

- Help by driving your companion to appointments, errands, etc.

- Support and accompany your companion in taking care of their basic needs of water, healthy food, exercise, and rest.

Chapter 6: Things That Can Hurt

- When people say or do hurtful things, they are usually displaying the ignorance and ineptitude around loss and grieving, not ill intent.

- Extend understanding and grace toward those who unintentionally offend.

Don'ts:

- Reacting derisively toward what seems odd or irrational behavior—be understanding of their mental state.

- Offering trite sayings or clichés—silence is better.

• Trivializing the loss—rule out saying anything that makes the loss seem less than it is or easier to endure or that is intended to make some kind of obvious sense of it.

• Expecting help or support—nobody should come to the grieving person to draw strength from them because, no matter how they seem, they are not available for that.

• Recommending, endorsing, or encouraging them to use work, busyness, recreation, entertainment, sex, drugs, alcohol, or any other substance or activity to numb or elude their pain; these are hindrances to a healthy recovery from grief, and they only delay the inevitable emotional avalanche.

• Rushing their grief—the one who grieves is entitled to however much time they need to recover fully.

Chapter 7: The Long Haul

• Grieving can take a long time, and we need friends for the long haul.

• Continue to care for the bereaved as you have from the outset.

- You can generally recognize when someone is making progress toward recovery.
- There are signs of a standstill or a recovery that has not started:
  - Attention-seeking
  - Self-medicating
  - Denying
  - Nursing negative emotions such as self-pity, anger, resentment, vindictiveness, jealousy, envy
- It's never too late to begin recovery, a healthy process of healing from grief.

Acknowledgments

I wish to thank those who read my drafts: my wife, Laura, friends Hannah Kolehmainen, Stewart Schlazer, Heather Brown, and Jill Rehkopf Smith; my mom, Jacqueline Rossini, and my uncle, Lawrence Rossini. Your encouragement and suggestions for improvement were invaluable.

Appreciation also goes to my kind and careful editor, Kristin Thiel, and to my patient and creative friend, Grant Hawley, who designed the cover.

This book could not have been produced without the generous support and assistance of all those who promoted and contributed to the Kickstarter campaign to launch this book. Much, much thanks to everyone.

All gratitude to our loving God, who has redeemed the sorrows of many, including mine, and and gently taught us the lessons that have made their way to these pages.

Resources

Online resources, current research, and contact information can appear, change, and disappear. Rather than publish a list of resources here that might soon become outdated, I have done so on the website for this book, www.atalossbook.com. Not only can I update current information as needed, I can add new resources as I become aware of them, and readers can alert me to resources they have found useful.

I also have an author website with information about my other projects.

You can contact me at either of these sites.
—SD

www.atalossbook.com

www.stevedehner.com

GREENTOWN PRESS
FOREST GROVE, OREGON

31814311R00052

Made in the USA
Middletown, DE
02 January 2019